# Instant HTML5 Geolocation How-to

Learn how to create elegant, location-aware web applications using the JavaScript Geolocation API

**Ben Werdmuller**

BIRMINGHAM - MUMBAI

# Instant HTML5 Geolocation How-to

First published: May 2013

Production Reference: 1160513

Published by Packt Publishing Ltd.
Livery Place
35 Livery Street
Birmingham B3 2PB, UK.

ISBN 978-1-78216-590-3

www.packtpub.com

# Credits

**Author**

Ben Werdmuller

**Reviewers**

Mark DuBois

Matt West

**Acquisition Editor**

James Jones

**Commissioning Editor**

Sharvari Tawde

**Technical Editor**

Prasad Dalvi

**Project Coordinator**

Suraj Bist

**Proofreader**

Ting Baker

**Cover Image**

Shantanu Zagade

**Production Coordinator**

Aparna Bhagat

**Cover Work**

Aparna Bhagat

# About the Author

**Ben Werdmuller** is a web developer, product manager, and entrepreneur. He co-founded Elgg, an open source social networking platform used by organizations such as NASA, the World Bank, and Oxfam. Currently, he serves as the CTO of latakoo.com, an enterprise platform for sending, storing, and sharing videos and large files. He writes at benwerd.com.

I'd like to thank my family, and the web community. My career, let alone this book, wouldn't have been possible without both of them. I'm on an incredible journey, and I'm forever grateful.

# About the Reviewers

**Mark DuBois** has been working with HTML since 1992. He built his first commercial website in 1995. Mark created the first accredited AAS degree in Web Systems and the first accredited certificate in rich Internet application development. Mark teaches many courses in web technologies at Illinois Central College. He has developed over 20 semester-long classes on various aspects of web design, development, and application security. His focus is on industry best practices regarding such items as security, accessibility, and web standards in these courses. He also serves as Director of Education for WebProfessionals.org and is recognized by Adobe as an Adobe Education Leader. Mark has recently taught numerous classes on HTML5, CSS3, and development of mobile apps using PhoneGap. He helps run both the Illinois and national web design contests for WebProfessionals.org (under the auspices of SkillsUSA). He can be found on Twitter (@Mark_DuBois) and posts articles on various aspects of web technology at http://blog.markdubois.info and http://blog.learning-html5.info.

**Matt West** is a developer and entrepreneur from Northampton, England. He previously founded the web development agency Developer City and is a contributor to a number of open source projects. Matt is currently working at his latest company, Koji Labs, which aims to create technological solutions for some of the world's biggest problems.

Matt is also the author of *HTML5 Foundations* (Wiley, 2012) and writes a blog at codingskyscrapers.com. You can find him on twitter as @MattAntWest.

# www.PacktPub.com

## Support files, eBooks, discount offers and more

You might want to visit www.PacktPub.com for support files and downloads related to your book.

Did you know that Packt offers eBook versions of every book published, with PDF and ePub files available? You can upgrade to the eBook version at www.PacktPub.com and as a print book customer, you are entitled to a discount on the eBook copy. Get in touch with us at service@packtpub.com for more details.

At www.PacktPub.com, you can also read a collection of free technical articles, sign up for a range of free newsletters and receive exclusive discounts and offers on Packt books and eBooks.

http://PacktLib.PacktPub.com

Do you need instant solutions to your IT questions? PacktLib is Packt's online digital book library. Here, you can access, read and search across Packt's entire library of books.

## Why Subscribe?

- ▶ Fully searchable across every book published by Packt
- ▶ Copy and paste, print and bookmark content
- ▶ On demand and accessible via web browser

## Free Access for Packt account holders

If you have an account with Packt at www.PacktPub.com, you can use this to access PacktLib today and view nine entirely free books. Simply use your login credentials for immediate access.

# Table of Contents

# Preface

Welcome to *Instant HTML5 Geolocation How-to*. This guide will help you make any web application aware of a user's location, quickly and easily. You will learn how to map a user's geographic location, integrate with popular mapping platforms, and track the user over time. In the process, you will create a simple application that generates a KML file containing both a path and points that you choose to save along that path (which can then be imported into Google Maps).

The iPhone changed the way we use the web. It was the first mobile device that included web browsing as a primary function. Suddenly, with mobile data and a phone like the iPhone, the web could be in your pocket, wherever you went. Through HTML5 and APIs, web applications could be truly context sensitive; they could know where you were, if you wanted them to, and react accordingly.

The Geolocation API is not part of HTML5, and is, instead, a JavaScript API standard. However, it sits alongside the evolving HTML5 specification as an important part of any modern web development toolkit.

## What this book covers

*Understanding the Geolocation API (Simple)* discusses how the JavaScript Geolocation API works, when you should use it, and how it is implemented in different browsers and on different devices.

*Setting up the application (Simple)* explains how to configure and set up a sample application layout suitable for running a simple Geolocation-aware web application. Each step is explained in a way that will help you understand how your data will be stored so that you can scale your application when you're ready.

*Getting the user's location (Intermidiate)* illustrates how to detect Geolocation support in the user's web browser, use the API to obtain the user's coordinates, and handle any errors that might occur.

*Displaying the user's location using the Google Maps API (Intermidiate)* discusses how to display the coordinates obtained in the previous section in a visual way using Google Maps.

*Displaying the user's location using a KML feed (Intermidiate)* explains how to create the KML feed from coordinates you have saved in previous sections, and test it by importing it into Google Maps. KML feeds are supported by popular mapping applications such as Google Maps and Google Earth, as well as specialist GIS software.

*Tracking and updating the user's location (Intermidiate)* illustrates how to track the user and show his/her path, using simple web technologies. Sometimes, tracking the user's movements is important. Here we will use `watchPosition()` and `clearPosition()` to track the user's location over time, and change the maps that were created in the previous section.

# What you need for this book

You need to have access to a server or computer running Apache Web Server, MySQL, and PHP. You will also need a text editor, a recent version of a major web browser, and optionally, a web-capable mobile device with GPS support.

# Who this book is for

*Instant HTML5 Geolocation How-to* is for web developers who want to incorporate Geolocation technology into their applications. There is no need to know anything about Geolocation software or standards; each section has been designed to help you understand how the API works from beginning to end. However, this book assumes a general understanding of web technologies, and both JavaScript and jQuery in particular.

# Conventions

In this book, you will find a number of styles of text that distinguish between different kinds of information. Here are some examples of these styles, and an explanation of their meaning.

Code words in text are shown as follows: "In this section, we will be concentrating on `index.php` and `callback.php`."

A block of code is set as follows:

```php
[<?php

$server = '';        // Enter your database server here
$username = '';       // Enter your database username here
$password = '';       // Enter your database password here
$database = '';       // Enter your database name here


// Connect to the database
```

**New terms** and **important words** are shown in bold. Words that you see on the screen, in menus or dialog boxes for example, appear in the text like this: "Select **File** | **Save** in your web browser while viewing the feed."

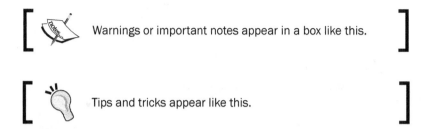

Warnings or important notes appear in a box like this.

Tips and tricks appear like this.

# Reader feedback

Feedback from our readers is always welcome. Let us know what you think about this book—what you liked or may have disliked. Reader feedback is important for us to develop titles that you really get the most out of.

To send us general feedback, simply send an e-mail to feedback@packtpub.com, and mention the book title via the subject of your message.

If there is a book that you need and would like to see us publish, please send us a note in the **SUGGEST A TITLE** form on www.packtpub.com or e-mail suggest@packtpub.com.

If there is a topic that you have expertise in and you are interested in either writing or contributing to a book, see our author guide on www.packtpub.com/authors.

# Customer support

Now that you are the proud owner of a Packt book, we have a number of things to help you to get the most from your purchase.

## Downloading the example code

You can download the example code files for all Packt books you have purchased from your account at http://www.PacktPub.com. If you purchased this book elsewhere, you can visit http://www.PacktPub.com/support and register to have the files e-mailed directly to you.

# Errata

Although we have taken every care to ensure the accuracy of our content, mistakes do happen. If you find a mistake in one of our books—maybe a mistake in the text or the code—we would be grateful if you would report this to us. By doing so, you can save other readers from frustration and help us improve subsequent versions of this book. If you find any errata, please report them by visiting http://www.packtpub.com/support, selecting your book, clicking on the **errata submission form** link, and entering the details of your errata. Once your errata are verified, your submission will be accepted and the errata will be uploaded on our website, or added to any list of existing errata, under the Errata section of that title. Any existing errata can be viewed by selecting your title from http://www.packtpub.com/support.

# Piracy

Piracy of copyright material on the Internet is an ongoing problem across all media. At Packt, we take the protection of our copyright and licenses very seriously. If you come across any illegal copies of our works, in any form, on the Internet, please provide us with the location address or website name immediately so that we can pursue a remedy.

Please contact us at copyright@packtpub.com with a link to the suspected pirated material.

We appreciate your help in protecting our authors, and our ability to bring you valuable content.

# Questions

You can contact us at questions@packtpub.com if you are having a problem with any aspect of the book, and we will do our best to address it.

# Instant HTML5 Geolocation How-to

Welcome to *Instant HTML 5 Geolocation How-to*. This guide will help you make any web application aware of a user's location, quickly and easily. You will learn how to map a user's geographic location, integrate it with popular mapping platforms, and track the user over time. In the process, you will create a simple application that generates a KML file containing both a path and points that you choose to save along that path (which can then be imported into Google Maps).

The iPhone changed the way we use the web. It was the first mobile device that included web browsing as a primary function. Suddenly, with mobile data and a phone like the iPhone, the web could be in your pocket, wherever you went. Through HTML5 and APIs, web applications could be truly context sensitive; they could know where you were, if you wanted them to react accordingly.

The Geolocation API is not part of HTML5, and is, instead, a JavaScript API standard. However, it sits alongside the evolving HTML5 specification as an important part of any modern web development toolkit.

## Understanding the Geolocation API (Simple)

At its core, the Geolocation API is a series of simple JavaScript calls that retrieve the following aspects of the user's location:

- Latitude and longitude
- Altitude
- The accuracy of the latitude and longitude

- ▸ The accuracy of the altitude information
- ▸ Heading
- ▸ Speed

It's worth noting that because of the aforementioned differences in technical capabilities, not all of these values are always available, even when the Geolocation API is working perfectly. For example, a laptop does not know what its altitude is. This is because it determines location in a different way, for example, to a smartphone with GPS access. These differences are discussed in the next section.

## How to do it...

The web can be accessed from different types of hardware, such as desktop computers, laptops, tablets, phones, and embedded systems.

 The **World Wide Web Consortium** (**W3C**) finalizes specifications in such a way that the web continues to support each of these platforms. Your operating system, Internet service provider, device type, and location all should not matter; the web is universal.

All of this means that the web may be the most important publishing medium in the history of human civilization—a medium that anyone can publish to and consume. However, because each device has slightly different capabilities, each feature may have slightly different characteristics from user to user. For example, in HTML5, some web browsers can play certain video formats, while other web browsers can play other video formats. In the Geolocation API, these changes relate to how location is computed, and as a result, how accurate it is.

Here's how the Geolocation API works from the user's perspective. You can see it in action by visiting my demo at `http://benwerd.com/lab/geo.php`.

1. Visit an application or website that requires location information.
2. The application attempts to determine your location with the Geolocation API.
3. The browser asks you whether you want to reveal the location to the application.
4. If you consent to sharing your location, your location is determined using available hardware and software, and sent to the application.
5. If you do not consent to sharing your location, no location information is sent to the application, and it is notified that no location information will be sent.

Your application needs the Geolocation API if:

- ▸ You want to adjust the application's functionality based on the user's location
- ▸ You want to adjust a site's content or redirect the user based on his/her location
- ▸ You want to empower the user to track his/her location over time

Your application cannot use the Geolocation API if:

- ▸ You want to track the user without his/her explicit consent
- ▸ You need real-time, extremely accurate location information

We will discuss why in the next section.

## How it works...

The request for information is an important step to protect user privacy. The Geolocation API specification explicitly states, "User Agents must not send location information to Web sites without the express permission of the user." It's sadly true that the user's location can often still be determined without his/her consent through other means, such as IP geolocation or by sharing data between applications. However, these are unrelated to the Geolocation API, and we will not be discussing them here.

Here's what a location request looks like when using Google Chrome on my MacBook Pro using a home broadband Internet connection:

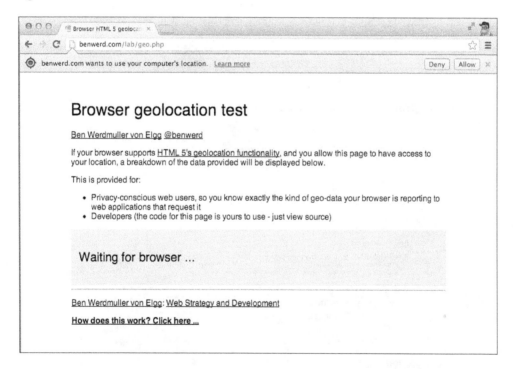

Note the ribbon above the main web page content. The entire content of the page has been sent to the browser; once location information has been sent, JavaScript could change the content of the page (for example, using the jQuery framework), submit the content elsewhere using a callback, or forward the browser to another page.

Here's what it looks like in the Android Chrome browser:

You can test your browser's geolocation capabilities by visiting `http://benwerd.com/lab/geo.php`.

Here's what it looks like when using Google Chrome on my MacBook Pro using cable Internet:

Here you can see that although my latitude and longitude have been calculated reasonably accurately, my altitude, heading, and speed details are not available. This is because these details are determined using **GPS** (**Global Positioning System**) technology, and my laptop does not have this capability. Instead, my web browser needs to guess my location based on various environmental factors.

Here's what the same Geolocation API test looks like on my Android Chrome browser on my cell phone:

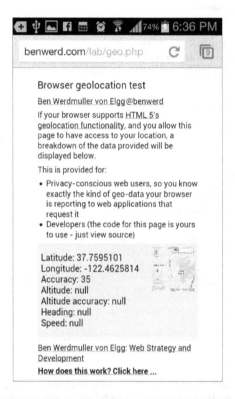

You might be surprised to see that my altitude, heading, and speed information is still not present, despite having been determined on a cellphone that has hardware GPS support. In fact, this is because (if you use the default Geolocation API configuration) Chrome on Android attempts to use WiFi location first, where it's available, before resorting to the relatively battery-intensive (but more accurate) GPS location.

Here's what the test page looks like on an iPad:

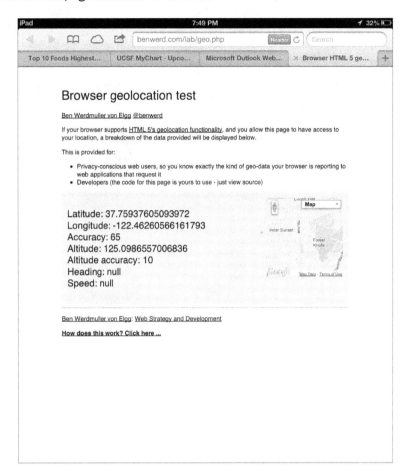

Because the iPad did use GPS data to determine my location, altitude information is available. However, I wasn't moving, so there's no speed or heading information.

Only latitude, longitude, and accuracy are guaranteed to be there. The other fields are entirely dependent on the user's device, movement, and location context.

Where GPS is not available, the browser will use a process called trilateration to determine the location.

Trilateration looks at environmental factors such as available wireless networks and their relative signal strengths, proximity to cellphone towers, and current network IP address, and matches them against a remote database of environmental factors against known locations. For most browsers, this database turns out to be run by Google, but some providers use a solution from Skyhook Wireless, and there are others too. Apple maintains its own database for its products, for example, which have probably been crowdsourced from consumer iPhone and iPad usage. Database information could also have been gathered from special cars, such as those used to take photographs for Google StreetView, and other crowdsourcing techniques. It's important to note that the user's location is being sent to a third party in these instances, and that the returned location will only be as good as the service's database. How this location is determined is not part of the Geolocation API specification; all that is required for you to know is that some location information is returned.

## There's more...

All modern browsers across both desktop and mobile platforms, except for Opera Mini, support the Geolocation API. Most have done so for enough time that you should be comfortable using the API in your web applications.

- ▶ Microsoft Internet Explorer from Version 9.0 onwards (March 14, 2010)
- ▶ Mozilla Firefox from Version 3.5 onwards (June 30, 2009)
- ▶ Google Chrome from Version 5.0 onwards (May 25, 2010)
- ▶ Android Browser from Version 2.1 onwards (January, 2010)
- ▶ Apple Safari on the desktop from Version 5.1 onwards (July 20, 2011)
- ▶ Apple Safari on iOS from Version 3.2 onwards (April 3, 2010)
- ▶ Opera from Version 10.6 onwards (July 1, 2010)
- ▶ BlackBerry Browser from Version 7.0 onwards (May, 2011)

(Source: `CanIUse.com`)

It's worth noting that because Microsoft Internet Explorer 9.0 was the first version to not support Windows XP, there remains a significant enterprise userbase—Internet Explorer users with Windows XP operating systems—that cannot use applications based on the Geolocation API. At the time of writing, this represents 24 percent of all web users worldwide according to `theie8countdown.com`. For this and a host of other reasons, including their own security, let's hope that they will upgrade soon.

The lack of Opera Mini support also means that many mobile phone users, particularly in developing nations or users with feature phones, are not able to use the Geolocation API. This situation is likely to change soon, as open source mobile operating systems such as Android and Firefox OS are gaining traction in those markets.

### Further resources

Here are some relevant resources for further research:

- **Can I Use Geolocation**: An up-to-date list of browsers that support the Geolocation API (`http://caniuse.com/#feat=geolocation`)
- **Geolocation API specification**: `http://dev.w3.org/geo/api/spec-source.html`

# Setting up the application (Simple)

In this section, we will learn which server software we require to support the Geolocation API, which server software we require to support the application we will build in this book, and how to set up your server software to support the application.

In this book, we're going to build a simple application that creates a **KML** (**Keyhole Markup Language**) feed of the user's movements that can be imported into mapping applications such as Google Maps and Google Earth. In order to do this, we need to capture the user's geolocation coordinates, save them into a database, and then export the saved coordinates into a data feed.

## Getting ready

There are four core actions that will need to be supported:

- Displaying the page containing the Geolocation API code
- Capturing the user's location
- Storing the user's location
- Displaying the user's history of locations as a KML feed

For the purposes of this book, we will support them in turn with:

- Apache Web Server
- Client-side JavaScript using jQuery (the Geolocation API itself requires no support on the server side; we'll use jQuery to simplify AJAX queries and manipulating content on the page)
- A MySQL database and the PHP scripting language
- A simple feed script written in PHP

Note that you could use any web browser, any web scripting language, and virtually any database, to perform these tasks. I hope that the examples here are generalized enough to allow you to translate them into the languages and server software of your choice. For example, if PHP isn't to your taste, these examples should be relatively easy to translate into Ruby or Python.

We will assume that you are running a recent copy of Apache Web Server, configured to allow scripting using PHP 5.3 or later.

## How to do it...

Create the following files in a new location on your web server:

- `index.php`: The main page that retrieves the user's location
- `callback.php`: The code that our JavaScript will call behind the scenes to save the user's location
- `feed.php`: The script that will echo the KML feed
- `lib.php`: A common file to handle the database connection and any other configuration
- `live.php`: A version of the main page that continuously retrieves the user's location
- `livepath.php`: A version of the main page that continuously retrieves the user's location and displays his/her route as a path

Create a new MySQL database table (and, if you like, a new database to house it in) for this example. This will store our retrieved geolocation coordinates, with a timestamp and an identifier for the user.

There are a number of different ways we could store the location information. Geolocation coordinates are returned as longitude and latitude; an angle on the surface of the Earth east and west of the Prime Meridian, and an angle north and south of the Equator, respectively. Recall the example data in the *Understanding the geolocation API (Simple)* recipe, the angles were returned to 14 decimal places. The more accurately we can store these numbers, the more accurately we can retrieve the user's location.

For the purposes of this tutorial, we are going to store our coordinates as a set of floating point numbers. This is because we're not performing any comparisons on the geographic data; we're simply storing and retrieving it.

All we need, then, is decimal point latitudes and longitudes with the required level of accuracy, as well as an integer identifier for the user, and another for the timestamp. As we'll be searching by user and timestamp, it's a good idea to maintain an index for each of these fields.

We'll call our database table `points`:

```
--
Table structure for table 'points'
--

CREATE TABLE IF NOT EXISTS 'points' (
'id' int(11) NOT NULL AUTO_INCREMENT COMMENT 'Our primary index
field',
'latitude' float NOT NULL COMMENT 'Our latitude coordinate',
'longitude' float NOT NULL COMMENT 'Our longitude coordinate',
'user_id' int(11) NOT NULL COMMENT 'The unique ID of the user',
'time' int(11) NOT NULL COMMENT 'The UNIX timestamp of the time when
the point was recorded',
PRIMARY KEY ('id'),
KEY 'user_id' ('user_id'),
KEY 'time' ('time')
) ENGINE=InnoDB;
```

**Downloading the example code**

You can download the example code files for all Packt books you have purchased from your account at http://www.PacktPub.com. If you purchased this book elsewhere, you can visit http://www.PacktPub.com/support and register to have the files e-mailed directly to you.

Note that I've also included a unique identifier for each row in the database, for ease of access later.

## There's more...

One of the problems with geographic data is that it's very easy to store a huge amount of it, which can cause databases to slow down if you're not careful—particularly, if you're doing a lot of proximity queries, for example, to discover stored geographic points within a certain radius of a location. The mathematics behind this functionality, while not massively complicated, can become expensive in aggregate.

MySQL has a spatial support extension, which allows you to store, retrieve, and compare extensions based on an optimized geographic engine. This uses a standard set from the OpenGIS project to store sets of geographic data. It's often installed by default, and is worth getting to know for more sophisticated geo-aware applications.

# Getting the user's location (Intermediate)

In this section, we will detect geolocation support, use the Geolocation API to obtain the user's coordinates (if we can), save the coordinates to MySQL via our PHP callback, and handle any errors that might occur.

## Getting ready

Make sure you've set up the required files in the previous section: index.php to serve the main page, callback.php to serve as our callback, and feed.php to serve as our KML feed. In this section, we will be concentrating on index.php and callback.php.

## How to do it...

Perform the following steps for getting the user's location:

1. First, set up lib.php as discussed here. This will be the file that handles connections to the database for all components in the system.

2. Fill in the blanks at the top of the page with your own database details. Note that for simplicity, I have used the built-in MySQL functions. For a fully fledged PHP application, I recommend using the built-in PDO library.

```php
<?php

$server = '';          // Enter your database server here
$username = '';             // Enter your database username here
$password = '';             // Enter your database password here
$database = '';          // Enter your database name here

// Connect to the database

if (mysql_connect(
  $server,
  $username,
  $password
)) {
  mysql_select_db(
    $database
  );
} else {
  header($_SERVER['SERVER_PROTOCOL'] .
  ' 500 Internal Server Error', true, 500);
  echo "Could not connect to the database.";
  exit;
}
```

3. Then, set up `callback.php`. This will accept longitude and latitude data from our location detection page via an HTTP POST request, and save it to our database:

```php
<?php
// Load our common library file, and fail if it isn't present
require_once('lib.php');

// Check for the existence of longitude and latitude in our POST
request
// variables; if they're present, continue attempting to save
if (isset($_POST['longitude']) && isset($_POST['latitude'])) {
  // Cast variables to float
  (never accept unsanitized input!)
  $longitude = (float) $_POST['longitude'];
  $latitude = (float) $_POST['latitude'];
  // For now, let's hard-code the user identifier to "1" -
  we can
  // use PHP sessions and authentication to set this
  differently later
  // on
  $user = 1;
  // Set the timestamp from the current system time
  $time = time();
  // Put our query together:
  $query = "insert into points set 'longitude' =
  {$longitude},
  'latitude' = {$latitude},
  'user_id' = {$user},
  'time' = {$time}";
  // Run the query, and return an error if it fails
  if (!($result = mysql_query($query))) {
    header($_SERVER['SERVER_PROTOCOL'] .
    ' 500 Internal Server Error', true, 500);
    echo "Could not save point.";
    exit;
  }

}
```

4. Finally, set up `index.php`. This is the page that users will access directly:

```html
<!doctype html>
<html>
  <head>
    <title>
      Location detector
```

```
</title>

<!-- We're using jQuery to simplify our JavaScript DOM-
handling code -->
<script src="//code.jquery.com/
jquery-1.9.1.min.js"></script>

<script language="javascript">

  // This function is called when the Geolocation API
  successfully
  // retrieves the user's location
  function savePosition(point) {

    // Send the retrieved coordinates to
    callback.php via a POST
    // request, and then set the page content to
    "Location saved"
    // once this process is complete
    (or "We couldn't save your
    // location" if it failed for some reason)
    $.ajax({
      url: 'callback.php',
      type: 'POST',
      data:   {
        latitude: point.coords.latitude,
        longitude: point.coords.longitude
      },
      statusCode: {
        500: function() {
          $('#locationpane').html
          ('<p>We couldn\'t save your location.</p>');
        }
      }
    }).done(function() {
      $('#locationpane').html
      ('<p>Location saved.</p>');
    }).fail(function() {
      $('#locationpane').html
      ('<p>We couldn\'t save your location.</p>');
    });

  }

  // This function is called when there is a problem
  retrieving
```

```
        // the user's location (but the Geolocation API is
        supported in
        // his or her browser)
        function errorPosition(error) {
          switch(error.code) {

          // Error code 1: permission to access the user's
          location
          // was denied
          case 1: $('#locationpane').html
          ('<p>No location was retrieved.</p>');
          break;

          // Error code 2: the user's location could not be
          determined
          case 2: $('#locationpane').html
          ('<p>We couldn\'t find you.</p>');
          break;

          // Error code 3: the Geolocation API timed out
          case 3: $('#locationpane').html
          ('<p>We took too long
          trying to find your location.</p>');
          break;

          }
        }

      </script>

  </head>
  <body>

    <div id="locationpane">

      <p>
        Waiting for location ...
      </p>

    </div>

    <!-- We're including the Geolocation API code at the
    bottom of the page
    so that page content will have loaded first -->
    <script language="javascript">

      // First, check if geolocation support is available
      if (navigator.geolocation) {

        // If it is, attempt to get the current position.
```

```
          Instantiate
          // the savePosition function if the operation was
          successful, or
          // errorPosition if it was not.
          navigator.geolocation.getCurrentPosition
          (savePosition, errorPosition);

      } else {

          // If the browser doesn't support the Geolocation
          API, tell the user.
          $('#locationpane').html
          ('<p>No geolocation support is available.</p>');

      }

    </script>

  </body>
</html>
```

## How it works...

There are two large JavaScript blocks in `index.php`, which together interact with the Geolocation API. In the body of the page, we've included a simple `div` element with ID `locationpane`, which we'll use to give feedback to the user. Every time we give feedback, we do so by changing the HTML contents of `locationpane` to contain a paragraph with a different message.

In the header of the page, there are two functions: `savePosition` and `errorPosition`. `savePosition` will be called by the Geolocation API when a location is determined and `errorPosition` will be called when there has been an error determining the location.

`savePosition` takes a single `Position` object as its first parameter. This has the following properties:

- ▶ coords: An object encapsulating the location's coordinates, which in turn contains the following attributes:
    - ❑ `latitude`: This is the user's latitude in degrees. This is a double value.
    - ❑ `longitude`: This is the user's longitude in degrees. This is a double value.
    - ❑ `accuracy`: This is the margin of error, in meters. This can be a double or a null value.
    - ❑ `altitude`: This is the number of meters above the mathematically defined surface of the Earth. This can be a double or a null value.

- ❑ altitudeAccuracy: This is the margin of error for the altitude, in meters. This can be double or a null value.

- ❑ heading: This is specified in degrees, clockwise relative to true north. This can be a double or a null value.

- ❑ speed: This is meters per second. This can be a double or a null value.

- ▶ timestamp (DOMTimeStamp): This is the timestamp that the location was retrieved.

Note that on some systems in certain contexts, the location won't be determined at the time of request; instead, a cached version will be returned. This is why the timestamp is important. However, we will discard it here.

savePosition uses jQuery's AJAX function to take the latitude and longitude from the coords object and sends it to callback.php. It then checks the HTTP response code; if callback.php has returned an error 500, it tells the user that his/her location could not be saved. (More on this in a moment.)

Meanwhile, if there was an error determining the user's location with the Geolocation API, errorPosition is called. This takes a PositionError object as its parameter, which has the following properties:

- ▶ code (short): A numeric error code
- ▶ message (DOMstring): An internal error message

Rather than output message, which isn't intended for end users, errorPosition looks at the error code to determine what kind of feedback to provide to the user:

- ▶ Error code 1: The user denied the application's request to track his/her location
- ▶ Error code 2: The user's location could not be determined
- ▶ Error code 3: The Geolocation API timed out

At the bottom of the page is the code that actually runs the Geolocation API.

Before accessing the JavaScript API functions, it's important to check to make sure that the Geolocation API is supported in the current browser. To do this, you can simply check to make sure the navigator.geolocation object exists:

```
if (navigator.geolocation) { /* The Geolocation API is supported */ }
```

If it doesn't, we should give the user feedback to explain that his/her location cannot be determined. We could also attempt to retrieve the user's location using server-side technologies such as IP geolocation, but this is much less accurate and out of the scope of this book.

Once we're sure, we can use the Geolocation API, we can call `navigator.geolocation.getCurrentPosition`, with references to the success and failure functions as its parameters:

```
navigator.geolocation.getCurrentPosition(savePosition, errorPosition);
```

It's worth mentioning here that a third parameter is available, which takes a `PositionOptions` object. This may contain the following properties:

- `enableHighAccuracy`: This is a Boolean value. It enables high accuracy mode (default: `off`).

- `timeout`: This is a Boolean value. This is the threshold beyond which the API times out (in milliseconds; the default is no limit).

- `maximumAge`: This is a long value. The maximum age of a cached location that we'll accept, in milliseconds (default: `0`).

If we enable high accuracy mode, mobile devices with GPS units will attempt to use it to get the best possible location information (if their owner has allowed it); otherwise, they may default to using trilateration to determine the location. However, because not all devices have these units and because GPS signals are not always available, requesting the current position with high accuracy is more likely to fail.

While high accuracy, location detection will not automatically fall back to the standard method, you can achieve this yourself, if you like. First, call `getCurrentPosition` with `highAccuracy` set to `true` and with a reference to a new error handling function:

```
navigator.geolocation.getCurrentPosition(savePosition,
highAccuracyErrorPosition, {enableHighAccuracy: true});
```

All this new error handler, `highAccuracyErrorPosition`, does is call `getCurrentPosition` with `highAccuracy` set to `false`:

```
function highAccuracyErrorPosition(error) {

navigator.geolocation.getCurrentPosition(savePosition, errorPosition,
{enableHighAccuracy: false});

}
```

The result is that the browser attempts to use high-accuracy location detection, and falls back to the standard method if it is not available due to some reason. Should the user decline authorization for location information, this continues to be respected down the chain.

The callback script, `callback.php`, first loads the database functionality from `lib.php` and ensures that it can connect. If connection fails for some reason, it returns an HTTP error 500 (Internal Server Error), which tells `index.php` to display an error to the user, as previously described.

If `callback.php` is connected to the database successfully, it then sanitizes the input variables, `latitude` and `longitude`. It's important to make sure both are cast to floating point variables, to minimize the risk of SQL injection attacks. The script also retrieves the current UNIX epoch timestamp (represented as the number of seconds since 00:00 on January 1, 1970).

The script makes it possible to store location information for an unlimited number of users. However, because authentication and user handling are not within the scope for this book, we've hardcoded the user's unique ID to 1. If you had a separate MySQL user table, for example, you would set this value to the ID of the currently logged-in user. This ID would be saved in the current browser session at the point of login. `callback.php` would use the version saved in the session rather than sent to it explicitly via a GET or POST variable, to prevent third parties from maliciously saving location information to a user's account.

Finally, `callback.php` attempts to save this data to the MySQL table we created in the previous section, using a standard MySQL insert call:

```
$query =      "insert into points set 'longitude' = {$longitude},
        'latitude' = {$latitude},
        'user_id' = {$user},
        'time' = {$time}";
```

Once again, if an error occurs, the script returns an HTTP 500 error so that the JavaScript on `index.php` can let the user know in a friendly way.

Otherwise, we can reasonably assume that the data was saved in our MySQL table. Because we saved it with timestamp information, and because we are also saving the user's unique ID in the same table row, we will be able to easily retrieve any individual user's locations in chronological order later on.

PHP's default HTTP response code is 200: OK. This tells the jQuery call in `index.php` that the positioning data was saved without any problems. In turn, `index.php` lets the user know that his/her location was saved.

## Displaying the user's location using the Google Maps API (Intermediate)

Now that we've written the code to save the user's location at a particular time, we need to consider how we'll display it. In this section, we'll use the Google Maps API to display the user's location right now, as well as recent locations that we've saved for this user.

The Google Maps API is the most popular online mapping API in the world, which is why we will use it for this tutorial. Other mapping APIs are available, including offerings from Microsoft Bing, Nokia, and the open source OpenStreetMap project. My decision to pick the Google Maps API does not reflect on the quality of these other APIs, and you will want to carefully choose between them based on their merits and applicability for your project. I have included links to these projects at the end of this section, as well as to the Google Maps API documentation.

Use of the Google Maps API is free for non-profit websites at the time of writing. Commercial sites are limited to 25,000 map loads per day. Beyond that, you will need to acquire a Google Maps API for Business license by contacting Google directly.

We will be using the Google Maps API v3 for the purposes of this tutorial.

## How to do it...

Let's begin by retrieving all of our previously-saved points.

1. First, alter `lib.php` as follows. Recall that this is the script file that connects to the database so that points can be saved. We're now expanding its role to include a helper function to retrieve all the previously saved points for a particular user.

```php
<?php

$server = '';            // Enter your database server here
$username = '';                // Enter your database username here
$password = '';                // Enter your database password here
$database = '';          // Enter your database name here

// Connect to the database server, and then select $database as
the database
if (mysql_connect   (
  $server,
  $username,
  $password
)) {
  mysql_select_db(
    $database
  );
} else {
  header($_SERVER['SERVER_PROTOCOL'] .
  ' 500 Internal Server Error', true, 500);
  echo "Could not connect to the database.";
  exit;
}
```

```php
/**
Retrieve all the stored locations in the database
@return array
*/
function getPreviousLocations($user_id) {

  // Initialize the array that we'll return
  $points = array();

  // It's always important to validate input,
  and particularly when
  // we're using it in the context of a database query.
  Here we make
  // sure $user_id is an integer.
  $user_id = (int) $user_id;

  // SQL query to simply return all points from our
  database - over time
  // you may wish to add a limit clause
  $query = "select 'latitude', 'longitude', 'time' from
  'points' where user_id = $user_id order by 'time' desc";

  // If we have points in the database, add them to the
  $points array
  if ($result = mysql_query($query)) {
    while ($row = mysql_fetch_object($result)) {
      $points[] = $row;
    }
  } else {
  echo mysql_error();
}
// Finally, return the $points array
return $points;


}
```

2. Then, expand `index.php` to load the Google Maps API, retrieve any previous points, and display both the set of previous location points and the current location on a map:

```php
<?php

// Load our common library file, and fail if it isn't present
require_once('lib.php');
```

```
?>
<!doctype html>
<html>
  <head>
    <title>
      Location detector
    </title>

    <!-- We're using jQuery to simplify our JavaScript
    DOM-handling code -->
    <script type="text/javascript"
    src="//code.jquery.com/jquery-1.9.1.min.js"></script>

      <!-- We're using the Google Maps API v3;
      note that we need to tell
      Google we're using a sensor for geolocation -->
      <script type="text/javascript"
      src="//maps.googleapis.com/maps/api/js?v=3.
      exp&sensor=true"></script>

      <script type="text/javascript">

        // This function is called when the Geolocation API
        successfully
        // retrieves the user's location
        function savePosition(point) {

          // Save the current latitude and longitude as
          properties
          // on the window object
          window.latitude = point.coords.latitude;
          window.longitude = point.coords.longitude;

          // Send the retrieved coordinates to callback.php
          via a POST
          // request, and then set the page content to
          "Location saved"
          // once this process is complete
          (or "We couldn't save your
          // location" if it failed for some reason)
          $.ajax({
            url: 'callback.php',
            type: 'POST',
            data:    {
```

```
                    latitude: window.latitude,
                    longitude: window.longitude
                },
                statusCode: {
                    500: function() {
                    $('#location_pane').html
                    ('<p>We couldn\'t save your location.</p>');
                    }
                }
            }
        }).done(function() {
            // Let the user know the location's been
            saved to the database
            $('#location_pane').html
            ('<p>Location saved.</p>');

            // Center the map on the user's current location
            var currentLocation =
            new google.maps.LatLng(window.latitude,
            window.longitude);
            window.googleMap.setCenter(currentLocation);

            // Create a marker at the user's current location
            var marker = new google.maps.Marker({
                position: currentLocation,
                map: window.googleMap,
                title: 'Current location'
            });
        }).fail(function() {
            $('#location_pane').html
            ('<p>We couldn\'t save your location.</p>');
        });

}

// This function is called when there is a problem
retrieving
// the user's location (but the Geolocation API is
supported in
// his or her browser)
function errorPosition(error) {
    switch(error.code) {

        // Error code 1: permission to access the user's
```

```
        location
        // was denied
        case 1: $('#location_pane').html('<p>No location was
        retrieved.</p>');
        break;

        // Error code 2: the user's location could not be
        determined
        case 2: $('#location_pane').html
        ('<p>We couldn\'t find
        you.</p>');
        break;

        // Error code 3: the Geolocation API timed out
        case 3: $('#location_pane').html
        ('<p>We took too long trying to find your
        location.</p>');
        break;

    }
}

// This function is called when there is a problem
retrieving
// The high-accuracy position. Instead of failing
outright, it
// attempts to retrieve the low-accuracy position,
telling the
// getCurrentPosition function to call errorPosition if
there is
// an error this time.
function highAccuracyErrorPosition(error) {

  navigator.geolocation.getCurrentPosition(savePosition,
  errorPosition, {enableHighAccuracy: false});

}

</script>

</head>
<body>
```

```html
<div id="location_pane">

  <p>
    Waiting for location ...
  </p>

</div>
<div id="map_pane" style="width: 500px;
height: 500px"></div>

<!-- We're including the Geolocation API code at the
bottom of the page
so that page content will have loaded first -->
<script language="javascript">

// Set initial viewing options for the map
var mapOptions = {
  zoom: 15,
  mapTypeId: google.maps.MapTypeId.HYBRID
};

// Initialize the map as a googleMap property on
the window object
window.googleMap =
new google.maps.Map
(document.getElementById('map_pane'), mapOptions);

// Load any previous points into a JSON array,
which itself is written
// to the page using PHP. We're hardcoding the user
ID to 1, as in
// callback.php.
var jsonPoints =
<?=json_encode(getPreviousLocations(1));?>;

// If jsonPoints isn't empty,
iterate through and create new map points
// for each geolocation point
if (jsonPoints.length > 0) {
  window.points = new Array();
  jsonPoints.forEach(function(point) {
    window.points.push(new google.maps.Marker({
      position: new google.maps.LatLng
      (point.latitude, point.longitude),
```

```
        map: window.googleMap
    })))
  });
}

// First, check if geolocation support is available
if (navigator.geolocation) {

  // If it is, attempt to get the current position.
  Instantiate
  // the savePosition function if the operation was
  successful, or
  // errorPosition if it was not.
  navigator.geolocation.getCurrentPosition
  (savePosition, highAccuracyErrorPosition,
  {enableHighAccuracy: true});

} else {

  // If the browser doesn't support
  the Geolocation API, tell the user.
  $('#location_pane').html
  ('<p>No geolocation support is available.</p>');

}

</script>

</body>
</html>
```

## How it works...

To display our location data, we will use a MySQL function stored in `lib.php` to retrieve existing map points. We will also load the Google Maps API using Google's hosted JavaScript library and make use of the following Google Maps objects:

- `Map`: The Google Map itself
- `Marker`: An individual point on a Google Map
- `LatLng`: An object representing a pair of latitude and longitude coordinates

There are three main structural changes we must make to `index.php`. First, we must require that `lib.php` is loaded. This will give us access to the database and a new function that we'll add to that library.

So far, we've only stored geolocation data; we haven't displayed it to the user at all. However, because we've been saving it to the database, we potentially have a rich history of location data that we can retrieve—organized by both user and time. A new function, `getPreviousLocations($user_id)`, returns this data as an array in chronological order using a simple MySQL select call:

```
$query = "select 'latitude', 'longitude', 'time' from 'points' where
user_id = $user_id order by 'time' asc";
```

Recall that for the purposes of this tutorial, we're always setting `$user_id` to 1. A more sophisticated application would substitute a user identifier from the current browser session, or another location.

By requiring `lib.php` at the top of `index.php`, we can ensure that we have reliable access to this information from the database:

```php
<?php
// Load our common library file, and fail if it isn't present
require_once('lib.php');
?>
```

Another new addition is the JavaScript library that Google provides for the Google Maps API. Note that by omitting the URI scheme (`http:` or `https:`), we can ensure that the browser will use the correct one, whether your page is accessed over a standard or secure HTTP connection. This is placed within the HTML `<head>` tag in `index.php`:

```
<script type="text/javascript" src="//maps.googleapis.com/maps/api/
js?v=3.exp&sensor=true"></script>
```

Finally, we also need a place on the page to display our map. For this, we establish a new, empty `div` element with a unique ID (here I've used `map_pane`). The Google Maps API will populate this with a complete map later.

Now that we've set up the framework of the page, we can begin configuring the map. We do this in the JavaScript block at the bottom of the page:

```javascript
// Set initial viewing options for the map
var mapOptions = {
  zoom: 15,
  mapTypeId: google.maps.MapTypeId.HYBRID
};
```

The zoom level for Google Maps starts at 0, where you can see the entire globe. Theoretically, the zoom levels are infinite, but in practice, for most maps, the maximum level is 19. Set the zoom level at 15; it's close enough to be able to view your location with precision, but zoomed out enough to see a large amount of the surrounding neighborhood.

There are a number of different map types at your disposal:

▶ `google.maps.MapTypeId.ROADMAP`: The street map view

▶ `google.maps.MapTypeId.SATELLITE`: A satellite view of the Earth

▶ `google.maps.MapTypeId.HYBRID`: Street map items overlaid on top of the satellite view

▶ `google.maps.MapTypeId.TERRAIN`: Terrain information without road markings and so on

For now, set the `mapTypeId` to `googlemaps.MapTypeId.HYBRID`.

Next, initialize the `Map` object with the options you've just defined, and the `map_pane` DOM element. This is enough to display the map inside the `map_pane` div. We'll save it to the `window.googleMap` global variable, which will come in handy.

```
window.googleMap = new google.maps.Map(document.getElementById('map_
pane'), mapOptions);
```

However, there's every chance we've already got some location information to display. Here's where our PHP function, `getPreviousLocations($user_id)`, becomes useful. Recall that it's returning an array of database row objects containing latitude, longitude, and time.

JavaScript is a front-end language, interpreted in the web browser; PHP is a server-side language, interpreted before any HTML is received by the browser. They cannot directly interface with each other. As a result, we need a way to pre-process the array of coordinates so that it's readable by JavaScript. JSON is perfect for this task.

Luckily, PHP provides a very simple function to encode PHP variables as `JSON`: `json_encode`. We just need to use this on the result of `getPreviousLocations($user_id)`. Remembering that we're hardcoding the value `1` in place of `$user_id`, our hybrid JavaScript/PHP code looks like the following:

```
var jsonPoints = <?=json_encode(getPreviousLocations(1));?>;
```

If there was a single location point in the database, this might be rendered as follows:

```
var jsonPoints = [{"latitude":"37.7595","longitude":"-
122.463","time":"1362975429"}];
```

In other words, `jsonPoints` is seen by JavaScript as an array of JavaScript objects. We can simply check that the array is non-empty, and iterate through any elements using the `Array.forEach` method:

```
if (jsonPoints.length > 0) {
  window.points = new Array();
  jsonPoints.forEach(function(point) {
    window.points.push(new google.maps.Marker({
```

```
      position: new google.maps.LatLng(point.latitude,
      point.longitude),
      map: window.googleMap
    }))
  });
}
```

We establish `window.points` as a global JavaScript array of Marker objects, the objects used to represent individual geographic points in the Google Maps API. On instantiation, Marker objects are given a position in terms of a LatLng object containing latitude and longitude, and a reference to the Google Map that will display them. (We can simply supply the `window.googleMap` variable we created earlier for this purpose.)

Once the previously saved geographic points have been written to the map, we must ensure that the newly detected location, if it has been successfully obtained, is also added.

Previously, we had written a message to the screen—Location saved—once a location had been successfully processed. Now, we need to also draw it to the map.

First, we create a new LatLng object containing the latitude and longitude of the newly saved location:

```
var currentLocation = new google.maps.LatLng(window.latitude, window.
longitude);
```

Next, we can center the map on it using the Map object's `setCenter` method:

```
window.googleMap.setCenter(currentLocation);
```

Finally, we create a new Marker object, containing a simple title, the newly created LatLng object, and a reference to our Map:

```
var marker = new google.maps.Marker({
  position: currentLocation,
  map: window.googleMap,
  title: 'Current location'
});
```

The location appears as a pin on the map, alongside previously saved locations.

## See also

- **Google Maps API**: https://developers.google.com/maps/
- **Microsoft Bing Maps API**: http://www.microsoft.com/maps/developers/web.aspx
- **Nokia Here API**: http://developer.here.com/
- **OpenStreetMap**: http://www.openstreetmap.org/
- **CloudMade**: http://cloudmade.com/

# Displaying the user's location using a KML feed (Intermediate)

The **Keyhole Markup Language** (**KML**) is an XML-based markup language suitable for defining geographic data. Alongside GeoRSS, it's one of two main XML-based standards that Google Maps supports. It was originally developed for using with Google Earth, which was known as **Keyhole Earth Viewer** until Google acquired it. Because multiple applications support KML files, it's a good way to easily export your geographic data.

## Getting ready

Perform the following steps:

1. Ensure that you have a recent version of PHP installed.

2. Check that DOM extension of PHP 5 is installed. Specifically, this will use the XML `DOMDocument` class. For most installations of PHP 5, this will be installed by default, but it's worth checking, as not all installations are the same. You can read information about the DOM extension at `http://php.net/manual/en/book.dom.php`.

3. You may also wish to install Google Earth in order to test your KML feed. The website for Google Earth is listed at the end of this section.

## How to do it...

Perform the following steps to display the user's location using a KML feed:

1. Set up `feed.php` as follows. This will retrieve the location items using the `getPreviousLocations($user_id)` function that we created in the *Displaying the user's location using the Google Maps API (Intermidiate)* recipe. Using the PHP DOM extension, it will create an XML feed in Keyhole Markup Language, which will encode the locations and timestamps of each saved point.

```php
<?php

// Load our common library file, and fail if it isn't present
require_once('lib.php');

// PHP's date function requires that the timezone is set. As I'm located on
// America's west coast, I'm setting this to America/Los_Angeles. You can
// also set this in your php.ini.
date_default_timezone_set('America/Los_Angeles');
```

```php
// Create a new XML file using PHP's DOM extension.
$feed = new DOMDocument('1.0','UTF-8');
$feed->formatOutput = true;

// Create a root node for the XML document.
$rootNode = $feed->appendChild($feed->createElementNS('http://
earth.google.com/kml/2.2', 'kml'));

// Create a document node inside the root node.
$documentNode = $rootNode->appendChild($feed-
>createElement('Document'));
$documentNameNode = $documentNode->appendChild($feed-
>createElement('name','Location detector feed'));

// Attempt to retrieve previous map points - and if they exist,
iterate
// through them. Note that we're hardcoding $user_id to 1; in more
complex
// implementations with user management, we might get $user_id
from the
// current user session.
if ($points = getPreviousLocations(1)) {
  foreach($points as $point) {
    // Each place is stored inside a Placemark tag
    $placeNode = $documentNode->appendChild
    ($feed->createElement('Placemark'));
    // We're going to use the timestamp of the saved
    // location as its title
    $nameNode = $placeNode->appendChild
    ($feed->createElement('name',date('r',$point->time)));
    // The actual coordinates are stored inside a Point tag
    $pointNode = $placeNode->appendChild
    ($feed->createElement('Point'));
    // Note that KML coordinates are longitude
    // then latitude!
    $coordinatesNode = $pointNode->appendChild
    ($feed->createElement('coordinates',
    $point->longitude . ',' . $point->latitude));
    // Each place also has an actual TimeStamp tag
    $timeNode = $placeNode->appendChild
    ($feed->createElement('TimeStamp', date('c',$point->time)));
  }
}
```

```
// Make sure browsers know to render the feed as XML
header('Content-type: text/xml');

// Write the feed content to the page
echo $feed->saveXML();
```

2.  Ensure that the resulting feed looks something like this in your browser:

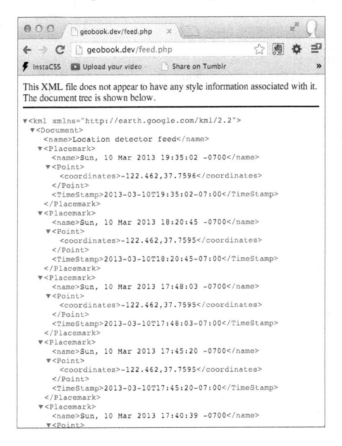

3.  If your feed is accessible to the public Internet, test it by entering its URL into the Google Maps search bar:

4.  Select **File | Save** in your web browser while viewing the feed, and save it with a filename ending in `.kml`.

5. You will be able to open the resulting KML file in Google Earth. If you have Google Earth installed, test the feed by double-clicking on the file.

## How it works...

It's not a good idea to hand-code an XML-based file, or to use a static template to do so. Various tools and libraries are available, and the DOM extension that was introduced with PHP 5 is an easy way to get started.

Our KML file consists of a Document node, which in turn contains a series of Placemark nodes. We could include a large amount of data here, but our minimum viable KML file will list name, timestamp, and geographic point information inside each Placemark. These are contained within name, TimeStamp, and Point nodes respectively. The Point node in turn contains a coordinates node, which lists the geographic coordinates of the point. Note that KML coordinates list the latitude first, followed by a comma, followed by the longitude. Spaces should not be used.

Placemarks can include more than one Point, as well as a selection of other geographic elements, but for the purposes of this example, we'll stick to one Point per Placemark.

TimeStamps are listed in ISO 8601 format. The TimeStamp for 7:30 p.m. Pacific Time on March 11, 2013 would appear as follows:

```
Mon, 11 Mar 2013 19:30:00 -0700
```

Create a new XML file in PHP by instantiating a DOMDocument object, specifying XML Version 1.0 and the UTF-8 character set:

```
$feed = new DOMDocument('1.0','UTF-8');
```

Define it as being a KML file by including the KML namespace, and establishing a root node:

```
$rootNode = $feed->appendChild($feed->createElementNS('http://earth.
google.com/kml/2.2', 'kml'));
```

New child nodes are added to a DOMDocument through use of the appendChild method; elements are created inside them using createElement. Now you have your root node, you can add the Document node:

```
$documentNode = $rootNode->appendChild($feed-
>createElement('Document'));
```

Using the getPreviousLocations function we created earlier, we can nest a series of Placemark nodes with the features as described in the preceding code line, using more calls to appendChild and createElement. The complete code is available in feed.php for you to peruse.

All of your data is now loaded into the feed. All that's left is to write it to the browser. First, you must tell it that this is an XML file, by setting the HTTP header appropriately:

```
header('Content-type: text/xml');
```

Finally, then, you can write it to the browser:

```
echo $feed->saveXML();
```

This is all you need to create a fully functional KML feed. There's much more available in the KML specification, including details about how to style map points, and other information that can be included inside the feed as a whole, as well as each individual Placemark. A link to the KML specification is included at the end of this section.

Because Google Maps natively supports KML, once you've made your system live on the web, you can simply paste the URL to your feed.php file into the Google Maps search box, and your geographic points will be displayed.

Additionally, you can choose to load your KML file into the map you created in index.php. This has the same effect as entering the address of your KML file into the Google Maps search bar, but on the map embedded in your own application.

You may remember that we created a global variable referencing the map called window. googleMap. Directly underneath, you can create a KmlLayer object as follows:

```
window.kmlLayer = new google.maps.KmlLayer('http://your/kml/feed.php');
window.kmlLayer.setMap(window.googleMap);
```

Of course, http://your/kml/feed.php must be replaced with the URL of your feed.

▸ **Keyhole Markup Language specification**: `https://developers.google.com/kml/`

# Tracking and updating the user's location (Intermediate)

While recording an individual location when the page loads is useful, in some situations you may wish to record the user's location continuously. The Geolocation API provides two functions for handling this use case—`watchPosition` and `clearWatch`—and in this section, we'll use them to modify our application to automatically resave the user's position when he/she moves.

## Getting ready

This section doesn't require any PHP programming; the modifications are all on the front end, using JavaScript. However, ensure that you have a compatible device with a GPS receiver and mobile data capability available to test your code. Most modern smartphones should suffice; we tested with the Chrome browser on a Samsung Galaxy S2, and in Safari on an iPhone 5.

## How to do it...

Perform the following steps to track and update the user's location:

1. Take a copy of `index.php`, and save it as `live.php`. We're going to modify it to use `watchPosition` and save multiple map points as follows:

```php
<?php
// Load our common library file, and fail if it isn't present
require_once('lib.php');

?>
<!doctype html>
<html>
<head>
<title>
Continuous location detector
</title>

<script type="text/javascript" src="//code.jquery.com/jquery-1.9.1.min.js"></script>
  <script type="text/javascript"
```

```
src="//maps.googleapis.com/maps/api/
js?v=3.exp&sensor=true"></script>

<script language="javascript">
```

This function is called when the Geolocation API successfully retrieves the user's location. Note that we are now saving our map points to an array:

```
function savePosition(point) {

  // Save the current latitude and longitude as properties
  // on the window object
  window.latitude = point.coords.latitude;
  window.longitude = point.coords.longitude;

  // Send the retrieved coordinates to
  callback.php via a POST
  // request, and then set the page
  content to "Location saved"
  // once this process is complete
  (or "We couldn't save your
  // location" if it failed for some reason)
  $.ajax({
    url: 'callback.php',
    type: 'POST',
    data:    {
      latitude: window.latitude,
      longitude: window.longitude
    },
    statusCode: {
      500: function() {
        $('#location_pane').html
        ('<p>We couldn\'t save your location.</p>');
      }
    }
  }).done(function() {
  // Let the user know the location's
  been saved to the database
  $('#location_pane').html('<p>Location saved.</p>');
  // Center the map on the user's current location
  var currentLocation = new
  google.maps.LatLng(window.latitude, window.longitude);
  window.googleMap.setCenter(currentLocation);
  // Create a marker at the user's current
  location and save it
```

```
    // to our array of map points
    window.geopath.push(new google.maps.LatLng(window.latitude,
window.longitude));
}).fail(function() {
$('#location_pane').html('<p>We couldn\'t save your location.</
p>');
});
}
```

This function is called when there is a problem retrieving the user's location (but the Geolocation API is supported in his/her browser):

```
function errorPosition(error) {
  switch(error.code) {
    // Error code 1: permission to access the user's
    location
    // was denied
    case 1: $('#location_pane').html('<p>No location was
    retrieved.</p>');
    break;
    // Error code 2: the user's location could not be
    determined
    case 2: $('#location_pane').html('<p>We couldn\'t find
    you.</p>');
    break;
    // Error code 3: the Geolocation API timed out
    case 3: $('#location_pane').html('<p>We took too long
    trying to find your location.</p>');
    break;
  }
}
```

2. And finally, add a function to prevent automatic updating of user location:

```
function stopWatching() {
  if (navigator.geolocation) {
    navigator.geolocation.clearWatch
    (window.watchLocationID);
    $('#watchingButton').hide();
  }
}
```

Following this, we move onto the body of the page, incorporating a new "stop watching" button:

```
</script>
</head>
```

```
<body>
  <div id="location_pane">
  <p>
    Waiting for location ...
  </p>
  </div>
  <p>
    <button onclick="stopWatching()"
    id="watchingButton">Stop watching position</button>
  </p>
    <div id="map_pane" style="width: 500px;
    height: 500px"></div>
    <!-- We're including the Geolocation API code
    at the bottom of the page
    so that page content will have loaded first -->
    <script language="javascript">
    // Set initial viewing options for the map
    var mapOptions = {
      zoom: 15,
      mapTypeId: google.maps.MapTypeId.HYBRID
    };

    // Initialize the map as a googleMap property
    on the window object
    window.googleMap = new
    google.maps.Map(document.getElementById('map_pane'),
    mapOptions);
    // Load any previous points into a JSON array,
    which itself is written
    // to the page using PHP. We're hardcoding
    the user ID to 1, as in
    // callback.php.
    var jsonPoints =
    <?=json_encode(getPreviousLocations(1));?>;
    window.polyLine = new google.maps.Polyline({
    strokeColor: '#ff0000',
    strokeOpacity: 1.0,
    strokeWeight: 3
  });
    window.polyLine.setMap(window.googleMap);
    window.geopath = window.polyLine.getPath();

    // If jsonPoints isn't empty, iterate through and
    create new map points
```

```
      // for each geolocation point
      if (jsonPoints.length > 0) {
        jsonPoints.forEach(function(point) {
          window.geopath.push(new google.maps.LatLng
          (point.latitude, point.longitude))
        });
      }
      // First, check if geolocation support is available
      if (navigator.geolocation) {
        // If Geolocation API support is available:
        // Attempt to get the current position, and
        // watch the user's location;
        instantiate the savePosition
        // function if the location was saved,
        or errorPosition if
        // it was not. Note that we don't ever want
        low-accuracy
        // location measurements in this context.
        window.watchLocationID =
        navigator.geolocation.watchPosition(savePosition,
        errorPosition, {enableHighAccuracy: true});
      } else {
        // If the browser doesn't support the
        Geolocation API, tell the user.
        $('#location_pane').html
        ('<p>No geolocation support is available.</p>');
      }
    </script>
  </body>
</html>
```

## How it works...

The Geolocation API watchPosition method uses a very similar syntax to the getCurrentPosition method we used earlier. Its parameters are the same:

- A callback function to call on success
- A callback function to call on failure
- An array of options

The available options, in turn, are also the same:

- enableHighAccuracy: This is a Boolean value, It enables high accuracy mode (default: off).

- timeout: This is a long value. It is the threshold beyond which the API times out (in milliseconds; the default is no limit).

- maximumAge: This is a long value. It is the maximum age of a cached location that we'll accept, in milliseconds (default: 0).

However, rather than initiating a single check for the user's location, it instead establishes a "watch" that will load the callback functions as appropriate whenever the device has detected that the user has moved. Because you need to reference the watch process, watchPosition returns an identifier.

The identifier is obtained when the method is called, as follows:

```
window.watchLocationID = navigator.geolocation.
watchPosition(savePosition, errorPosition, {enableHighAccuracy:
true});
```

Note that we've used the enableHighAccuracy option, while not failing back to a lower-accuracy location method. That's because in a situation where you're continually retrieving the location, low-quality data will not be useful. Because the device falls back to estimating location through environmental factors, visibly erroneous data may be included in your dataset, sometimes hundreds of meters or more away from the user's actual location, making it harder to track the user's path. It's better to fail if a GPS signal cannot be found.

Sometimes, the user may wish to switch tracking off, while remaining on the page. To do this, we've created a simple button. This will trigger the clearWatch method, which takes the watch process ID as a single parameter as follows:

```
navigator.geolocation.clearWatch(window.watchLocationID);
```

In our implementation, we've also hidden the button using the jQuery hide() method once it has been pressed.

Finally, our savePosition function, which is called whenever a new location is successfully received, must display the new location.

In our previous implementation, we simply created a variable for the new Marker object to display a single point. However, we also created a window.points array to keep the Marker objects that were reloaded from the database. In order to display the full set of points that are displayed as the user moves around, we'll need to add each newly created Marker in the array too.

To do this, we can just push new Marker objects to the array as follows:

```
window.points.push(new google.maps.Marker({
  position: currentLocation,
  map: window.googleMap,
  title: 'Detected location'
}));
```

However, a series of individual points isn't necessarily the best way to display this data.

## There's more...

Unfortunately, at the time of writing this book, there's no way to prevent the mobile device from switching its screen and GPS unit off. Consider the following screenshot from a walk I took around the Inner Sunset neighborhood in San Francisco:

Contrary to what the map might indicate, this was a continuous walk—I didn't suddenly leap two blocks in a single bound! However, while I was holding my device and ensuring that its screen didn't turn black on some of the streets (indicated by the vertical lines you can see here), on the others I chose to slip my device into my pocket, as an ordinary user might. The GPS receiver was deactivated automatically when the screen went black, in order to conserve battery life. As a result, no location points were saved for these portions of my journey.

We can further enhance our application by replacing the individual points on the map with a continuous line. This would also help smooth over any gaps in the dataset.

To achieve this, we need to replace the portions of the code that set points on the map using the Google Maps API. Google provides another element, `PolyLines`, which allows you to arbitrarily add coordinates to a continuous line. I've included the complete code as `livepath.php`.

In the portion of the page where we're setting up the map, just after we've loaded the `jsonPoints` JSON array, we need to create a polyline. We'll make it bright red (HTML color `#ff0000`) so that we can see it easily:

```
window.polyLine = new google.maps.Polyline({
  strokeColor: '#ff0000',
  strokeOpacity: 1.0,
  strokeWeight: 3
});
```

Now, we'll attach it to our existing map. `window.polyLine` will be the global variable that stores the polyline:

```
window.polyLine.setMap(window.googleMap);
```

And finally, we'll establish `window.geopath` as the array of points that make up the polyline. We're saving that as a global variable too, for convenience. You'll see why momentarily.

```
window.geopath = window.polyLine.getPath();
```

Now, let's load our JSON array of previously saved points onto it:

```
// If jsonPoints isn't empty, iterate through and create new map
// points for each geolocation point
if (jsonPoints.length > 0) {
  jsonPoints.forEach(function(point) {
    window.geopath.push(new google.maps.LatLng
    (
      point.latitude, point.longitude
    ))
  });
}
```

Finally, recall the AJAX done () function at the top of the page, which is called once a new location has been successfully processed. We can replace the Google Maps code in this function with a simple line to add the latest coordinates to our PolyLine:

```
// Create a marker at the user's current location and save it
// to our array of map points
window.geopath.push(new google.maps.LatLng(window.latitude, window.
longitude));
```

Now, whenever a new location is detected, it will be added to the line rather than to the map as a new, individual point.

The Geolocation API is an important addition to any modern web developer's arsenal. Together with other new APIs, HTML 5 itself and the new breed of mobile devices, the web doesn't just allow you to build high quality network applications; it allows you to build new kinds of context-aware applications that have never been created before. Happy building.

 **Thank you for buying**
# Instant HTML5 Geo-location How-to

# About Packt Publishing

Packt, pronounced 'packed', published its first book "*Mastering phpMyAdmin for Effective MySQL Management*" in April 2004 and subsequently continued to specialize in publishing highly focused books on specific technologies and solutions.

Our books and publications share the experiences of your fellow IT professionals in adapting and customizing today's systems, applications, and frameworks. Our solution based books give you the knowledge and power to customize the software and technologies you're using to get the job done. Packt books are more specific and less general than the IT books you have seen in the past. Our unique business model allows us to bring you more focused information, giving you more of what you need to know, and less of what you don't.

Packt is a modern, yet unique publishing company, which focuses on producing quality, cutting-edge books for communities of developers, administrators, and newbies alike. For more information, please visit our website: www.packtpub.com.

# Writing for Packt

We welcome all inquiries from people who are interested in authoring. Book proposals should be sent to author@packtpub.com. If your book idea is still at an early stage and you would like to discuss it first before writing a formal book proposal, contact us; one of our commissioning editors will get in touch with you.

We're not just looking for published authors; if you have strong technical skills but no writing experience, our experienced editors can help you develop a writing career, or simply get some additional reward for your expertise.

# HTML5 Mobile Development Cookbook

ISBN: 978-1-849691-96-3          Paperback: 254 pages

Over 60 recipes for building fast, responsive HTML5 mobile websites for iPhone 5, Android, Windows Phone, and Blackberry

1. Solve your cross platform development issues by implementing device and content adaptation recipes.

2. Maximum action, minimum theory allowing you to dive straight into HTML5 mobile web development.

3. Incorporate HTML5-rich media and geo-location into your mobile websites

# Responsive Web Design with HTML5 and CSS3

ISBN: 978-1-849693-18-9          Paperback: 324 pages

Learn responsive design using HTML5 and CSS3 to adapt websites to any browser or screen size

1. Everything needed to code websites in HTML5 and CSS3 that are responsive to every device or screen size

2. Learn the main new features of HTML5 and use CSS3's stunning new capabilities including animations, transitions and transformations

3. Real world examples show how to progressively enhance a responsive design while providing fall backs for older browsers

Please check **www.PacktPub.com** for information on our titles

## jQuery Mobile Web Development Essentials

ISBN: 978-1-849517-26-3          Paperback: 246 pages

Learn to use the touch-optimized, cross-device, cross-platform jQM web framework for smartphones and tablets

1. Create websites that work beautifully on a wide range of mobile devices with jQuery mobile

2. Learn to prepare your jQuery mobile project by learning through three sample applications

3. Packed with easy to follow examples and clear explanations of how to easily build mobile-optimized websites

## jQuery UI 1.8: The User Interface Library for jQuery

ISBN: 978-1-849516-52-5          Paperback: 424 pages

Build highly interactive web applications with ready-to-use widgets from the jQuery User Interface Library

1. Packed with examples and clear explanations of how to easily design elegant and     powerful front-end interfaces for your web applications

2. A section covering the widget factory including an in-depth example on how to build a custom jQuery UI widget

3. Updated code with significant changes and fixes to the previous edition

Please check **www.PacktPub.com** for information on our titles